ELEMENTARY+

Disney Heroines

10 PIANO ARRANGEMENTS IN PROGRESSIVE ORDER

CONTENTS

Disney Chararcters and Artwork © Disney

ISBN 978-1-70512-699-8

HAL•LEONARD®

Visit Hal Leonard Online at
www.halleonard.com

Contact us:
Hal Leonard
7777 West Bluemound Road
Milwaukee, WI 53213
Email: info@halleonard.com

In Europe, contact:
Hal Leonard Europe Limited
42 Wigmore Street
Marylebone, London, W1U 2RN
Email: info@halleonardeurope.com

In Australia, contact:
Hal Leonard Australia Pty. Ltd.
4 Lentara Court
Cheltenham, Victoria, 3192 Australia
Email: info@halleonard.com.au

Preface

The songs included in *Disney Heroines* represent a powerful message of courage and strength from a female perspective. These characters all dare to dream, to stand up, to overcome, to fight and reach beyond their circumstances to pursue their own happiness. No longer just a dependent princess seeking happiness from a prince, these heroines uncover their power by being independent, strong and secure for those they love. They question, they worry, they fall, but they put one foot in front of the other and do "The Next Right Thing." Be sure to ponder the lyrics of these amazing songs to reveal their deeper meaning. They can inspire us all to keep moving beyond whatever obstacles might be holding us back.

– Jennifer Linn

Jennifer Linn is a multi-talented pianist, composer, arranger and clinician. As a clinician, she has presented workshops, master classes, and showcases throughout the United States, Canada, and India. From 2009-2019 she held the title of Manager–Educational Piano for Hal Leonard LLC, the world's largest print music publisher. Ms. Linn is the editor and recording artist for the award-winning *Journey Through the Classics* series and the G. Schirmer Performance Editions of *Clementi: Sonatinas, Op. 36, Kuhlau: Selected Sonatinas*, and *Schumann: Selections from Album for the Young, Op. 68*. Her original compositions for piano students frequently have been selected for the National Federation of Music Clubs festival and other required repertoire lists worldwide.

Ms. Linn's teaching career spans more than 30 years and includes independent studio teaching of all ages, as well as group instruction and piano pedagogy at the university level. She received her B.M. with distinction and M.M. in piano performance from the University of Missouri–Kansas City (UMKC) Conservatory of Music where she was the winner of the Concerto-Aria competition. She was named the Outstanding Student in the Graduate piano division and given the prestigious Vice Chancellor's award for academic excellence and service. In 2013, the University of Missouri–Kansas City Conservatory of Music and Dance named Ms. Linn the UMKC Alumnus of the year. In 2020, she was presented with the Albert Nelson Marquis Lifetime Achievement Award as a leader in the fields of music and education.

About the Jennifer Linn Series

Each book in the *Jennifer Linn Series* will feature a wide variety of either original piano compositions or popular arrangements. The music is written in a **progressive order of difficulty**, so pianists of any age can enjoy their music with the added benefit of a gradual challenge as they advance to each new piece in the book. The *Jennifer Linn Series* includes five levels:

Early Bird books feature pre-staff notation with note names printed inside the note heads. The font size is large, and the book is in a horizontal format. Optional teacher or parent duets (in small font) are included. This level is for the beginner who has not yet learned to read notes on the staff.

Easy Elementary features the simplest, single-note Grand Staff notation in a large font size. This level is for the beginning pianist just learning to read notes on the staff and is printed in a regular vertical format.

Elementary+ books include melody with harmony for both hands and includes more rhythm choices and a larger range of keys. This book is for the progressing student who has two to three years of experience.

Easy Intermediate is similar to Hal Leonard's *Easy Piano* level but includes pianistic accompaniment patterns and more advanced rhythm notation as required.

Intermediate+ is for advancing pianists who have progressed to the Piano Solo level and enjoy lush accompaniments and stylistic original compositions and arrangements.

Show Yourself

from FROZEN 2

Music and Lyrics by Kristen Anderson-Lopez
and Robert Lopez
Arranged by Jennifer Linn

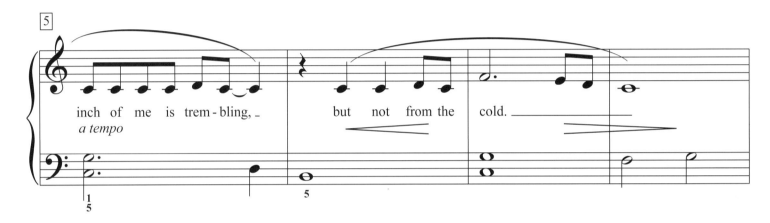

riv - ing, and it feels like I am home. I have

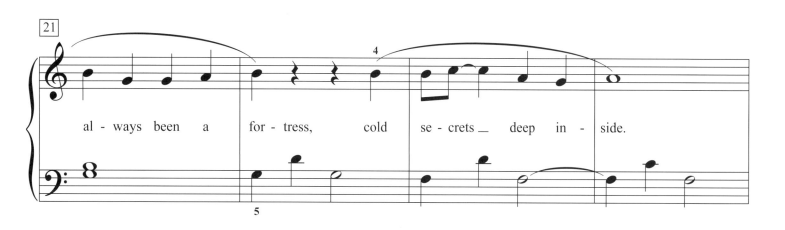

al - ways been a for - tress, cold se - crets__ deep in - side.

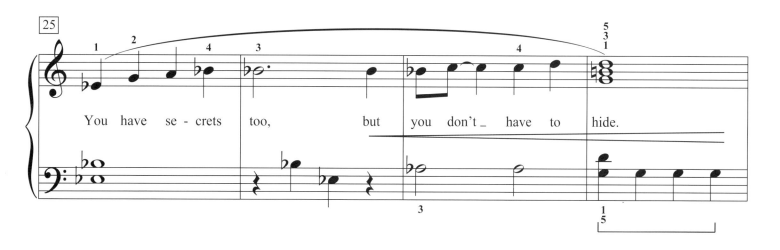

You have se - crets too, but you don't__ have to hide.

Show your-self: I'm dy-ing to meet___ you. Show your-self:

6

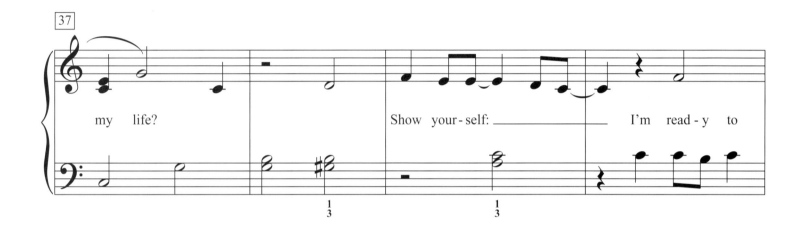

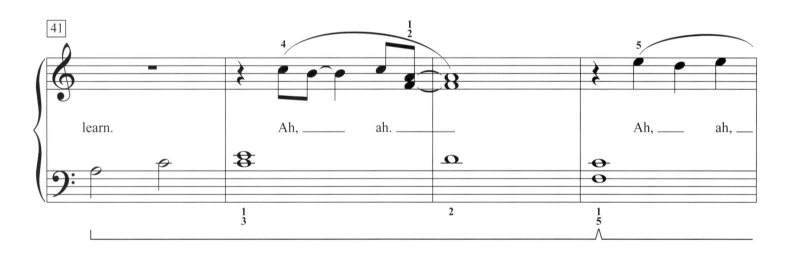

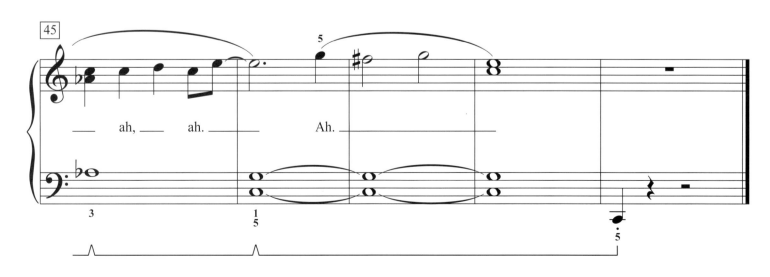

How Far I'll Go

from MOANA

Music and Lyrics by
Lin-Manuel Miranda
Arranged by Jennifer Linn

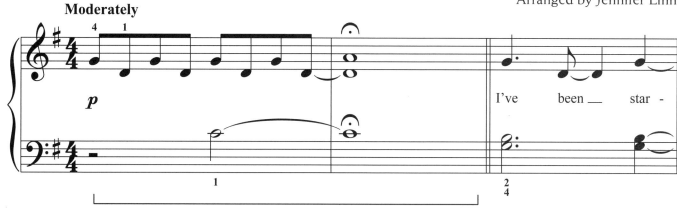

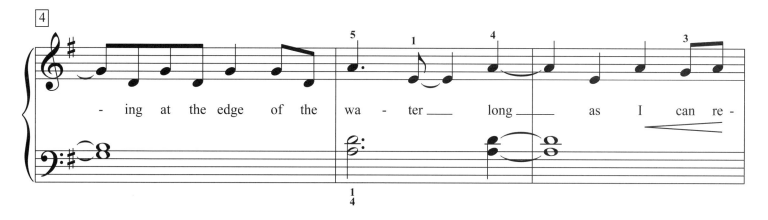

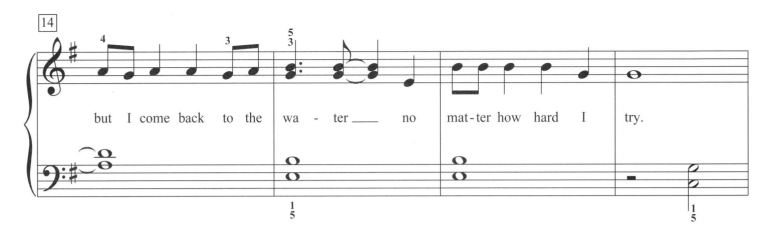

but I come back to the wa - ter ___ no mat-ter how hard I try.

Ev-'ry turn I take, ev-'ry trail I track, ev-'ry path I make, ev-'ry

mf

road leads back to the place I know where I can-not go, where I long to ___

be. See the line where the sky meets the sea, it calls ___

mp

_____ me, and no one knows _____ how far it

goes. _____ If the wind in my sail on the sea stays be-hind _____

_____ me, one day I'll know. _____ If I

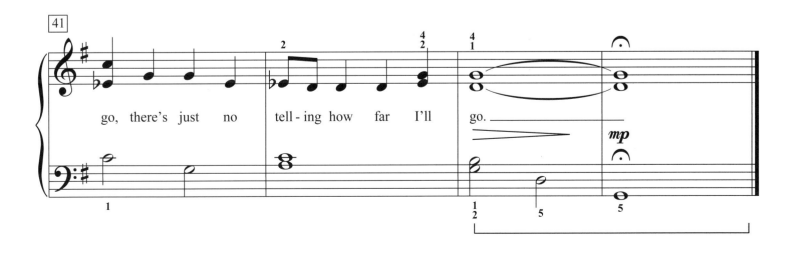

go, there's just no tell-ing how far I'll go. _____

Touch the Sky
from BRAVE

Music by Alexander L. Mandel
Lyrics by Alexander L. Mandel and Mark Andrews
Arranged by Jennifer Linn

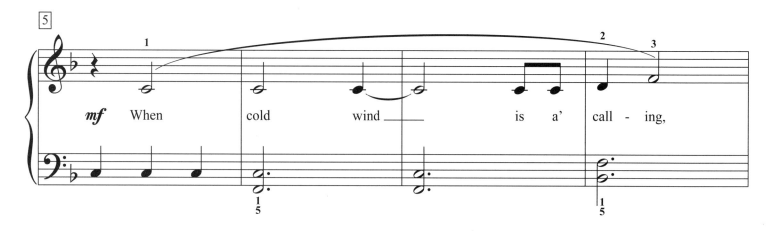

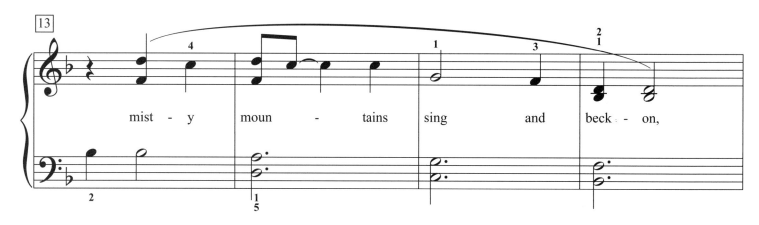

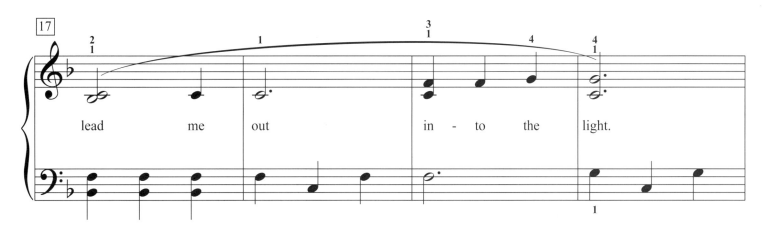

lead　　me　　out　　　　in - to　the　light.

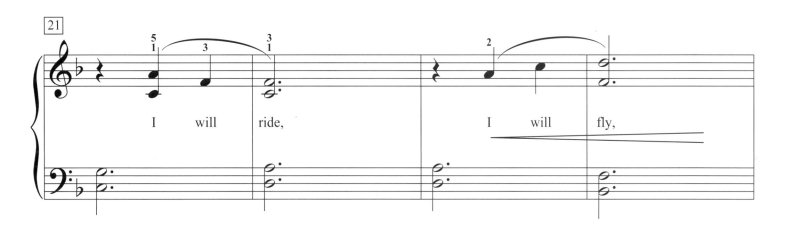

I　will　ride,　　　　　I　will　fly,

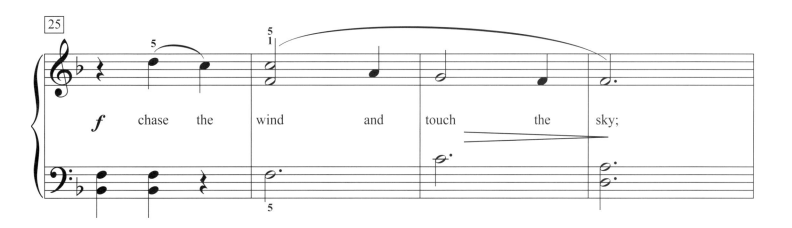

f chase　the　wind　and　touch　the　sky;

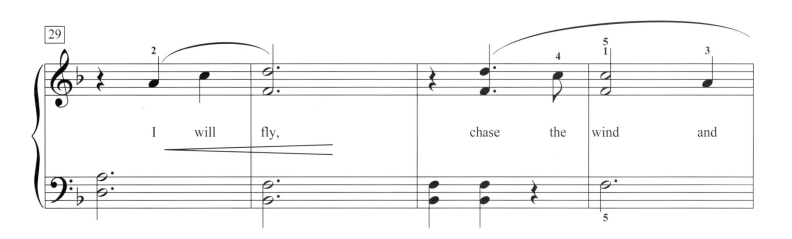

I　will　fly,　　　　chase　the　wind　and

touch the sky. Na na na na,

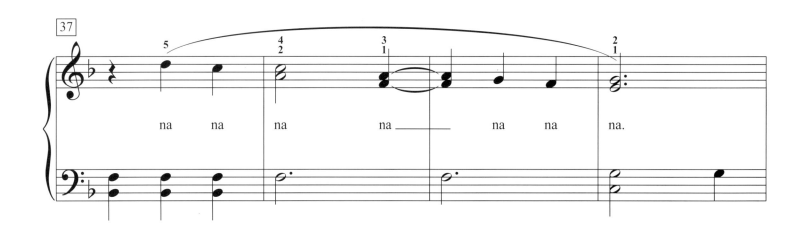

na na na na na na na.

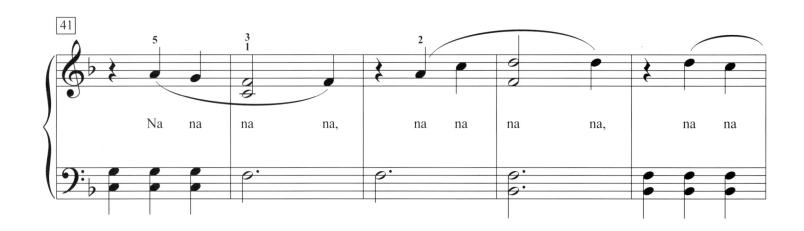

Na na na na, na na na na, na na

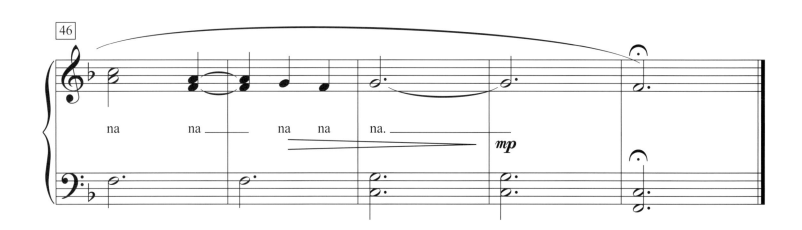

na na na na na.

mp

Part of Your World
from THE LITTLE MERMAID

Music by Alan Menken
Lyrics by Howard Ashman
Arranged by Jennifer Linn

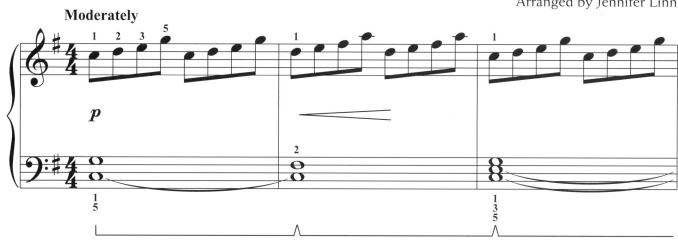

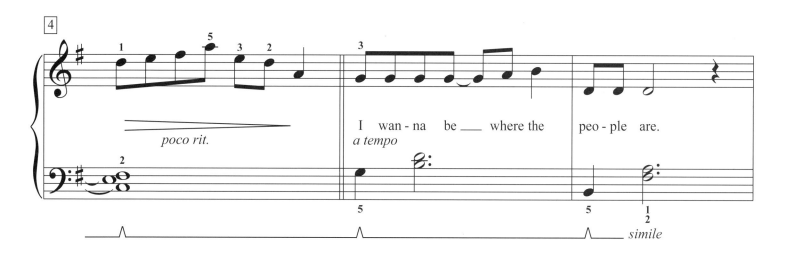

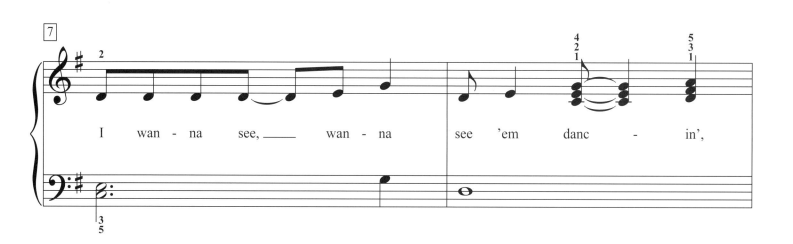

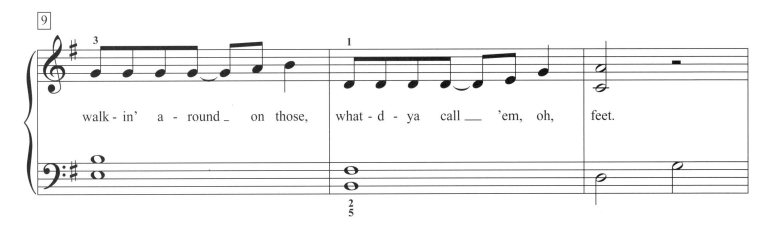

walk - in' a - round __ on those, what - d - ya call __ 'em, oh, feet.

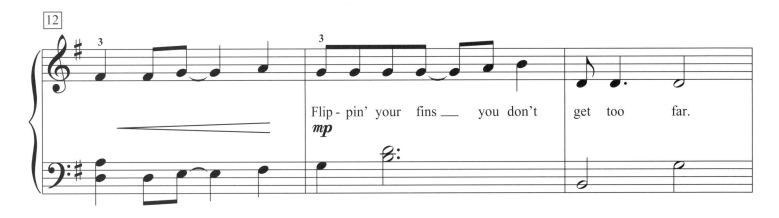

Flip - pin' your fins __ you don't get too far.
mp

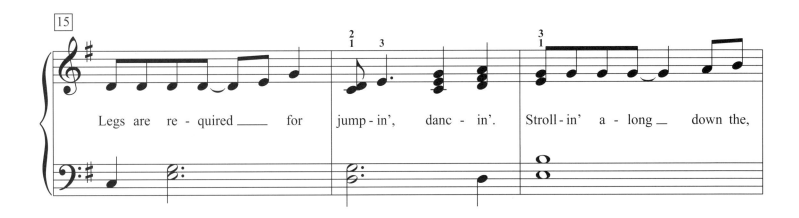

Legs are re - quired __ for jump - in', danc - in'. Stroll - in' a - long __ down the,

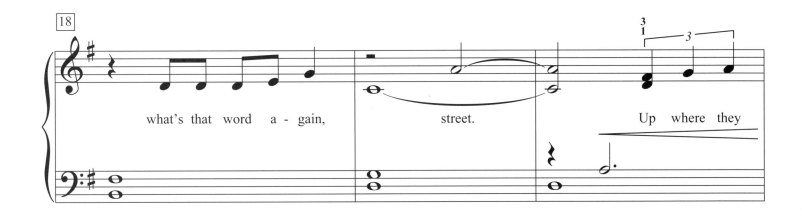

what's that word a - gain, street. Up where they

walk, up where they run, up where they stay all day ___ in the sun. ___

___ Wan - der - in' free, wish I could be part of that

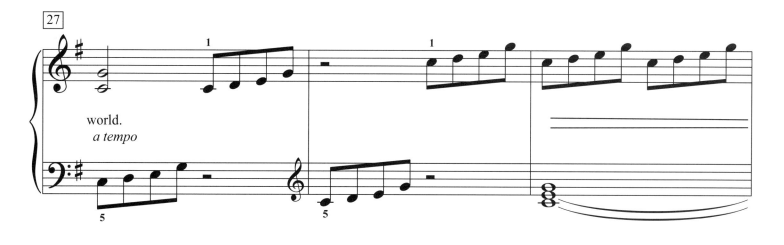

world. *a tempo*

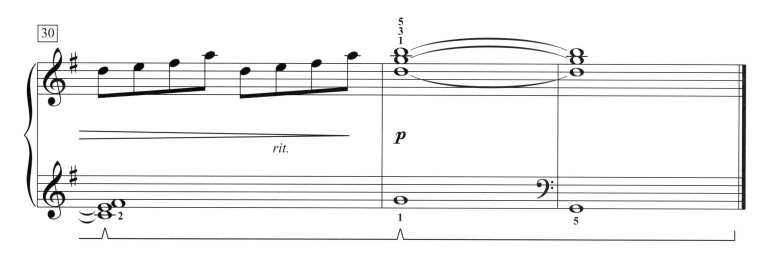

A Dream Is a Wish Your Heart Makes

from CINObrELLA

Music by Mack David and Al Hoffman
Lyrics by Jerry Livingston
Arranged by Jennifer Linn

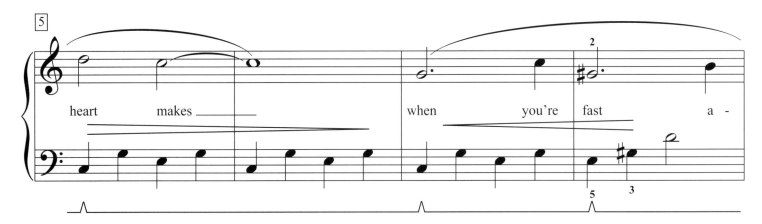

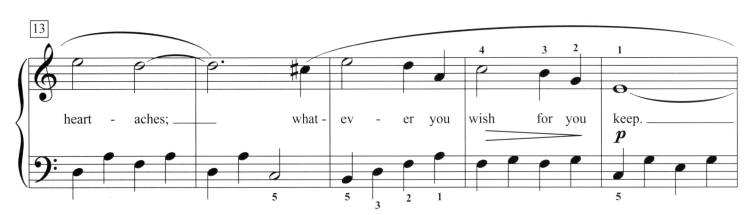

Have faith in your dreams and some - day your rain - bow will come smil - ing through. No mat - ter how your heart is griev - ing, if you keep on be - liev - ing, the dream that you wish will come true.

Reflection
from MULAN

Music by Matthew Wilder
Lyrics by David Zippel
Arranged by Jennifer Linn

Reflectively

Look at me, I will nev - er pass for a per-fect bride

or a per-fect daugh - ter. Can it be I'm not

meant to play this part?

Now I see that if I were tru - ly to be my - self,

simile

I would break my fam - 'ly's __ heart.

Who is that girl I see star - ing straight

back at me? Why is my re - flec - tion some - one

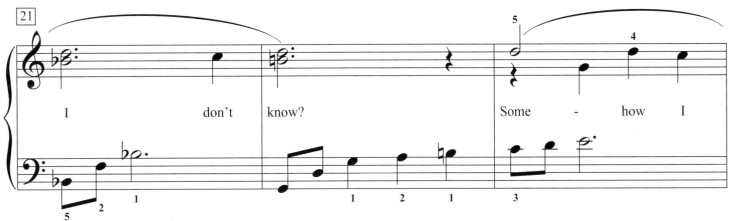

I don't know? Some - how I

can - not hide who I am, though I've tried.

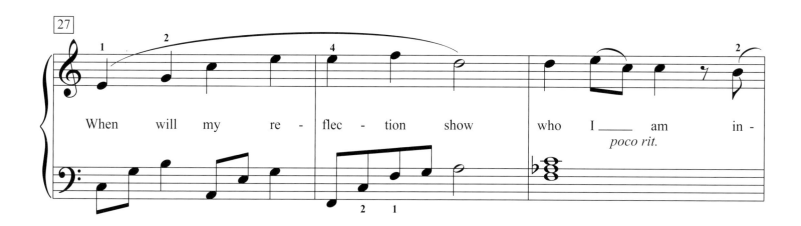

When will my re - flec - tion show who I ___ am in -

poco rit.

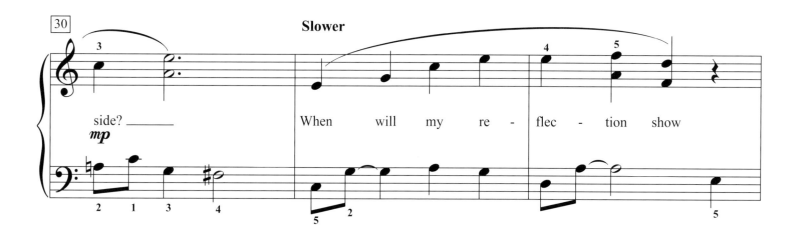

Slower

side? ___ When will my re - flec - tion show

mp

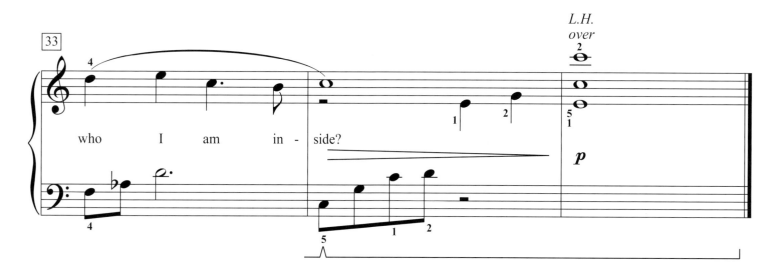

L.H.
over

who I am in - side?

p

This page has been intentionally left blank.

Almost There
from THE PRINCESS AND THE FROG

Music and Lyrics by
Randy Newman
Arranged by Jennifer Linn

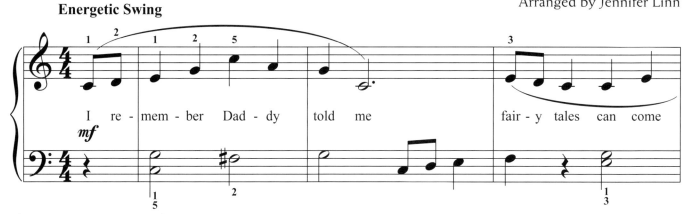

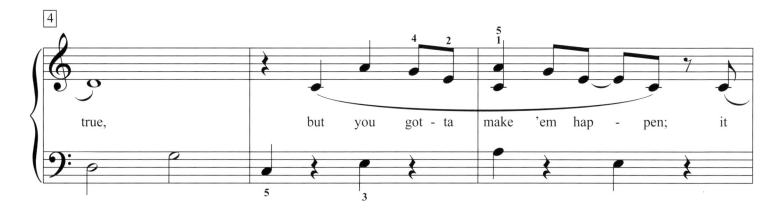

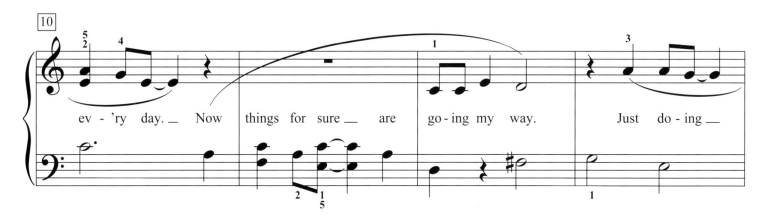

what I do, ___ look out, boys, ___ I'm com - in' through. _ And I'm

al - most there, I'm al - most

there. Peo - ple gon - na come here from ev - 'ry - where, _ and I'm

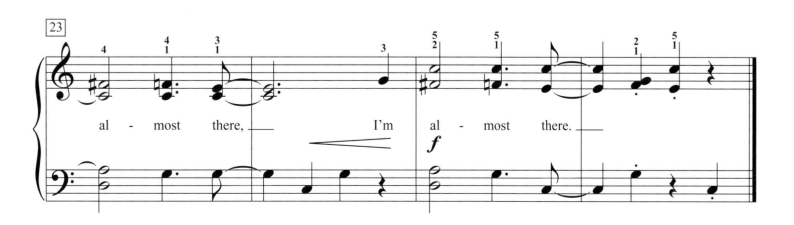

al - most there, ___ I'm al - most there. ___

Belle
from BEAUTY AND THE BEAST (2017)

Music by Alan Menken
Lyrics by Howard Ashman
Arranged by Jennifer Linn

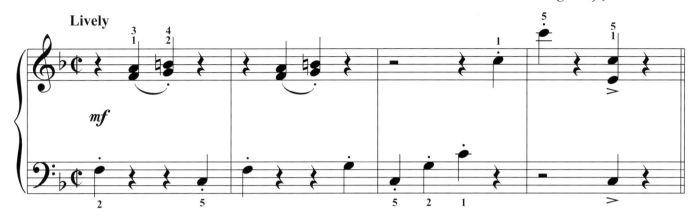

There goes the bak - er with his tray, like al - ways,

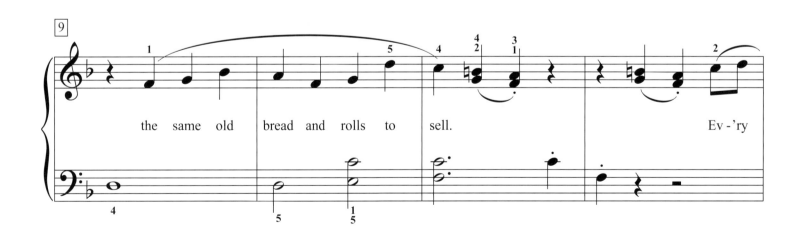

the same old bread and rolls to sell. Ev -'ry

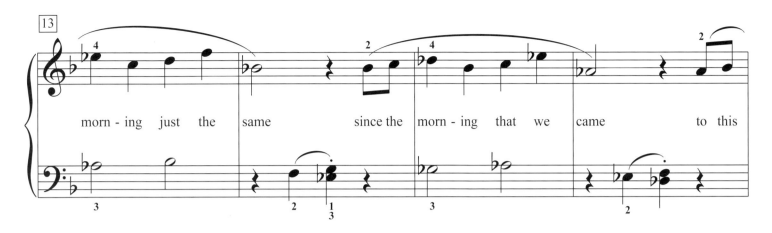

morn - ing just the same since the morn - ing that we came to this

poor pro - vin - cial town. *(Spoken:) Good morn - ing, Belle.*

R.H. soft & light

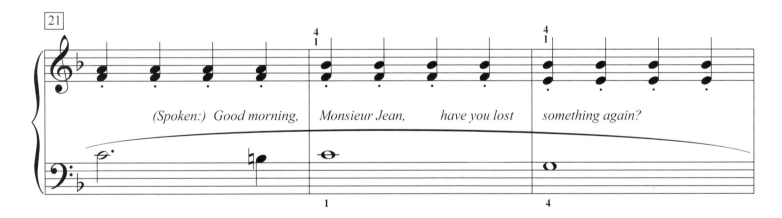

(Spoken:) Good morning, Monsieur Jean, have you lost something again?

Well, I believe I have. The problem is, I... can't remember what!

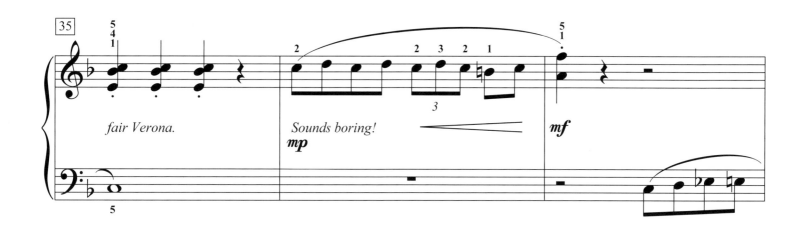

Dazed and dis - tract - ed, can't you tell? Nev - er

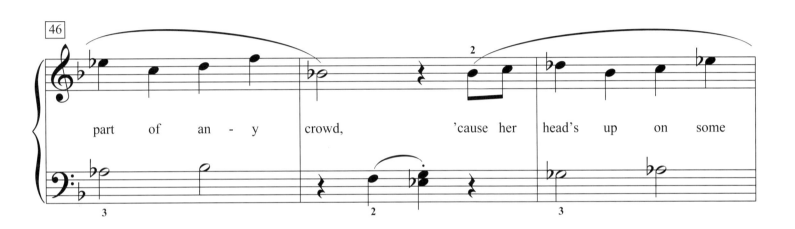

part of an - y crowd, 'cause her head's up on some

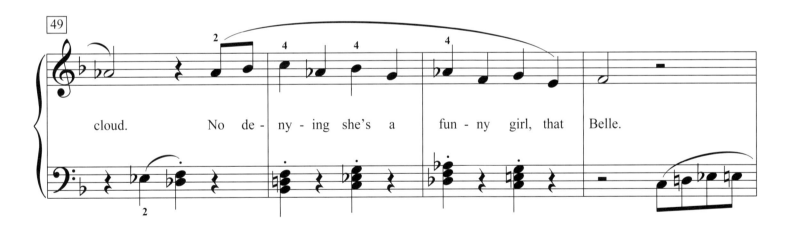

cloud. No de - ny - ing she's a fun - ny girl, that Belle.

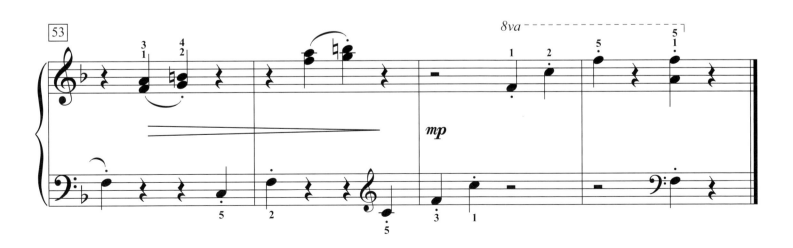

8va

mp

The Next Right Thing

from FROZEN 2

Music and Lyrics by Kristen Anderson-Lopez
and Robert Lopez
Arranged by Jennifer Linn

Just Around the Riverbend

from POCAHONTAS

Music by Alan Menken
Lyrics by Stephen Schwartz
Arranged by Jennifer Linn

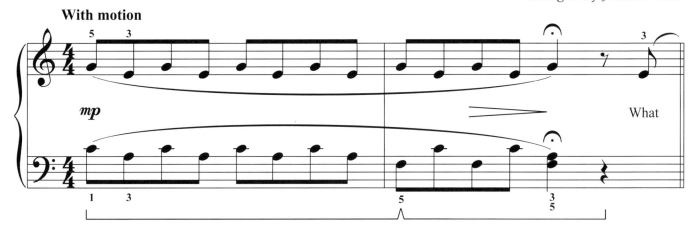

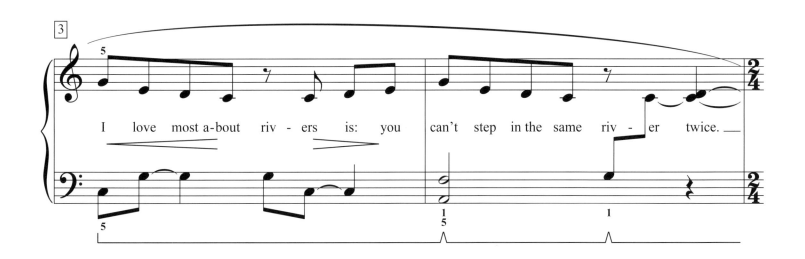

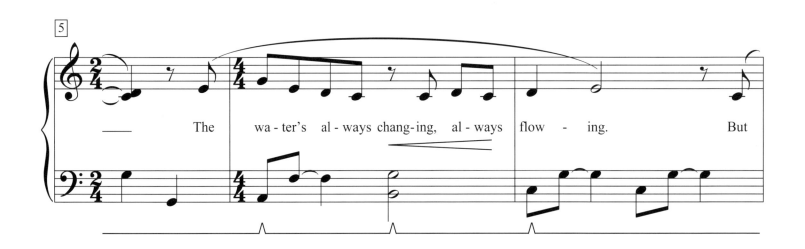

people, I guess, can't live like that; we all must pay a price: To be

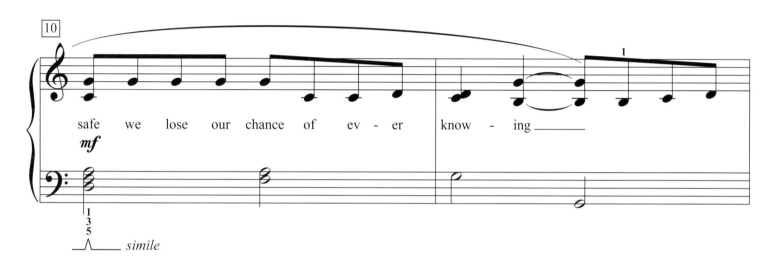

safe we lose our chance of ev - er know - ing ____

mf

simile

what's a - round the riv - er - bend, ____ wait - ing

just a - round ____ the riv - er - bend. I look once more

f

just a-round the riv-er-bend be-yond the shore, some-where past the sea. Don't

know what for... Why do all my dreams ex-tend just a-round the riv-er-bend?

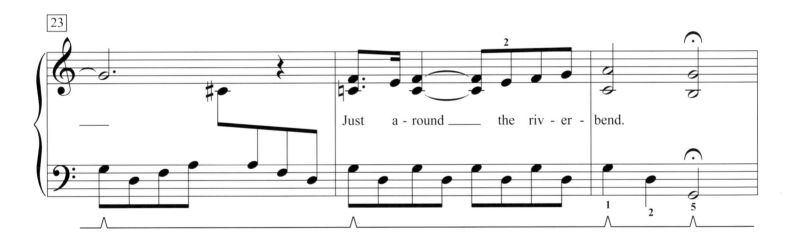

Just a-round the riv-er-bend.

molto rit. **pp**